O. C. E. LIBRARY

LIBRARY
WESTERN OREGON STATE COLLEGE
MONMOUTH, OREGON 97361

D0764431

Jeff's
Hospital
Book

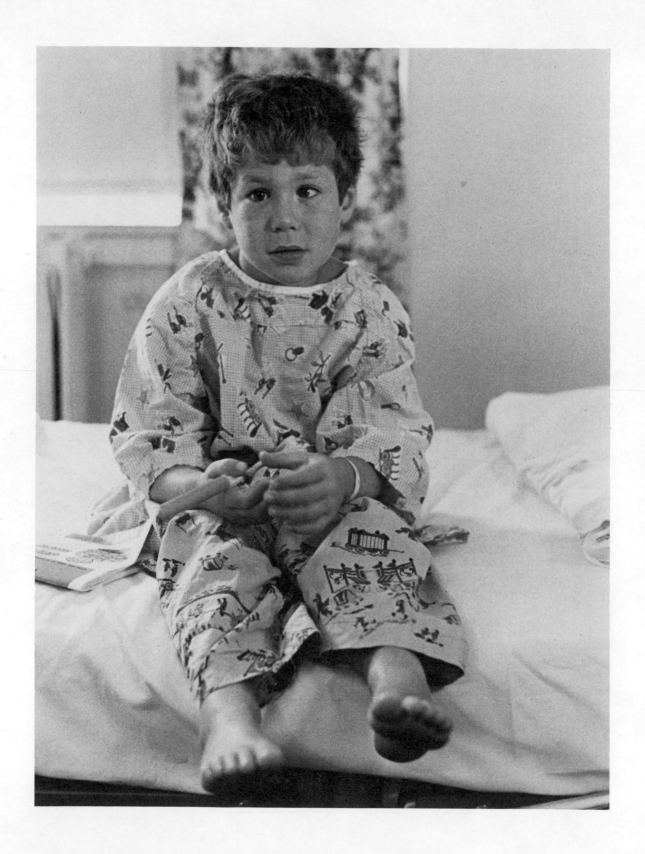

Jeff's Hospital Book

by Harriet Langsam Sobol

photographs by Patricia Agre

HENRY Z. WALCK, INC. New York

LIBRARY
WESTERN OREGON STATE COLLEGE
MONMOUTH, OREGON 97361

JUV.
RE
52
.S67
1975

#617.7
S

We wish to thank Dr. Richard Raskind, Assistant Clinical Professor of Ophthalmology, Cornell University Medical School, and Attending Surgeon, Manhattan Eye, Ear and Throat Hospital; and Dr. Nathaniel Donson, Instructor in Child Psychiatry, Columbia College of Physicians and Surgeons, and Consulting Psychiatrist, Department of Pediatrics, St. Luke's Hospital, for their invaluable participation in this story.

Text copyright © 1975 by Harriet Langsam Sobol
Photographs copyright © 1975 by Patricia Agre
All rights reserved
ISBN: 0-8098-1229-0
LC: 74-25982
Printed in the United States of America

10 9 8 7 6 5 4 3

Library of Congress Cataloging in Publication Data

Sobol, Harriet Langsam.

  Jeff's hospital book.

  SUMMARY: Describes a young boy's experience in the hospital as he undergoes surgery to correct crossed eyes.
    1. Eye—Surgery—Juvenile literature.   2. Children—Hospital care—Juvenile literature.   [1. Eye—Surgery.   2. Medical care.   3. Hospitals]   I. Agre, Patricia, ill.   II. Title.
RE52.S6   617.7′62   74-25982
ISBN 0-8098-1229-0

To
Alison
Alex
Andrea
Greg
Jenny
&
Jeff

Jeff's eyes had been crossed since he was a baby. His doctor finally decided that Jeff should have an operation that would make his eyes straight.

When the day came, Jeff and his mother went to the hospital early in the morning. Jeff ran ahead and waited at the hospital door.

Jeff had his favorite stuffed animal,
Walter, with him. As they waited, Jeff
felt afraid.

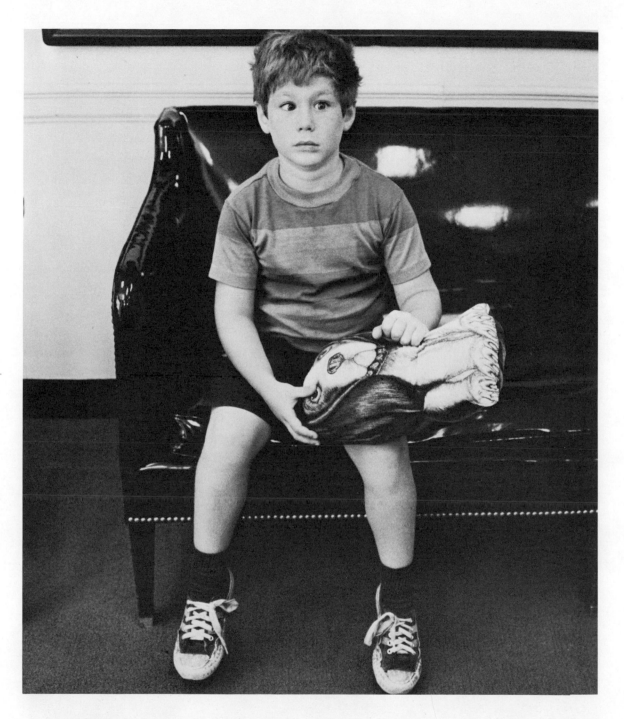

"Mrs. Langsam and Jeffrey," the
nurse called. "Please come to the
admissions desk."

The man at the admissions desk
asked Jeff's mother a lot of questions.
Jeff felt very lonely.

"Why are you putting the bracelet on me?" Jeff asked.

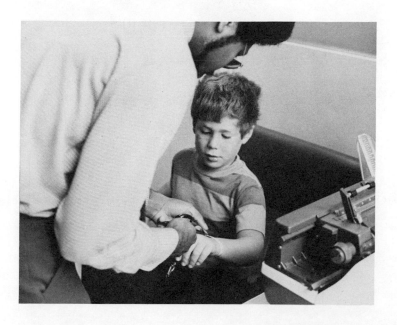

The man answered, "It has your name on it. Whenever a nurse comes to give you medicine she will look at your bracelet to make sure you're getting the medicine meant for you."

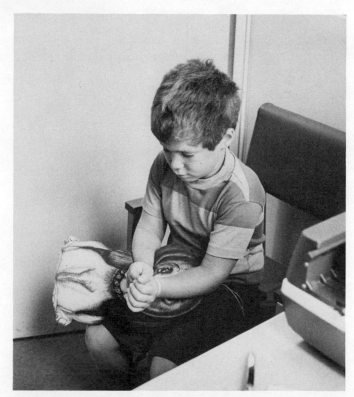

The man took Jeffrey and his mother to the laboratory so that a technician could give him a blood test.

"What are you putting on my finger?" Jeff asked.

"I'm cleaning it with alcohol and cotton."

"How big is the needle? Will it hurt?" Jeff asked.

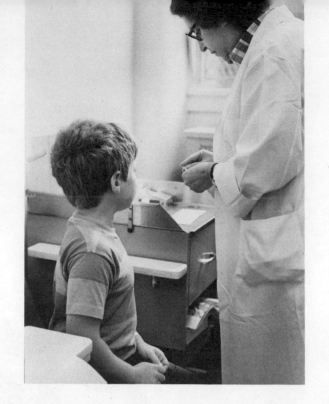

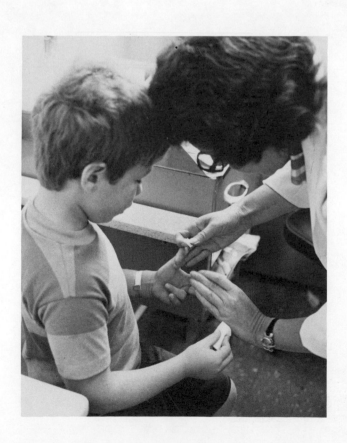

She showed him the little needle and said, "It will feel like a pinprick."

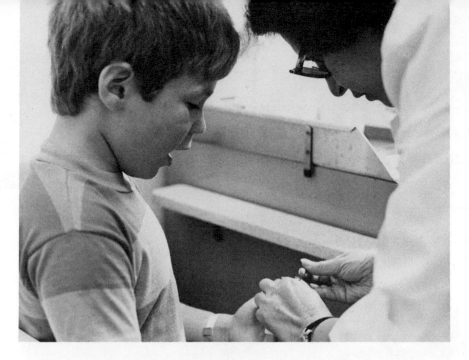

"Ouch, is that all? No more pricks? What are you doing now?"

"I'm just taking a little blood," she answered.

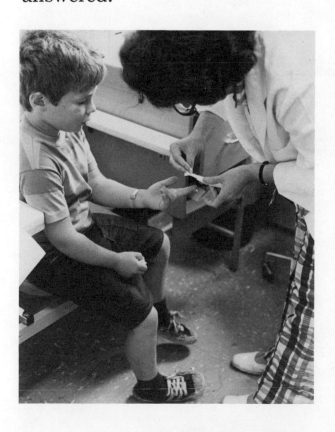

"Can I leave yet?" Jeff asked.

"In just a minute," the technician answered.

She put a Band-Aid on Jeff's finger and said good-by. She told Jeff and his mother to take the elevator up to the eighth floor.

On the eighth floor, the nurse showed them to Jeff's room. She looked at his bracelet to make sure he was "Jeff Langsam."

She told him to get into his pajamas. Jeff took his pajamas out of his suitcase and changed in the bathroom.

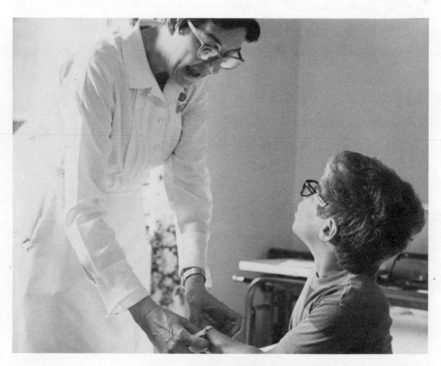

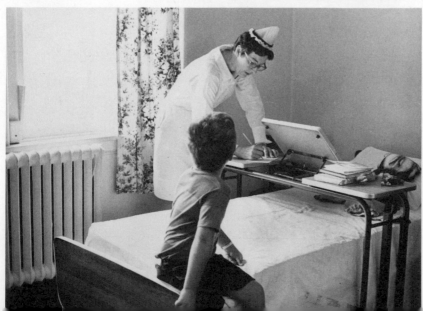

A nurse's aide came in and weighed
him. She took his pulse and his
temperature. She told him to go into
the bathroom and urinate into a
little jar.

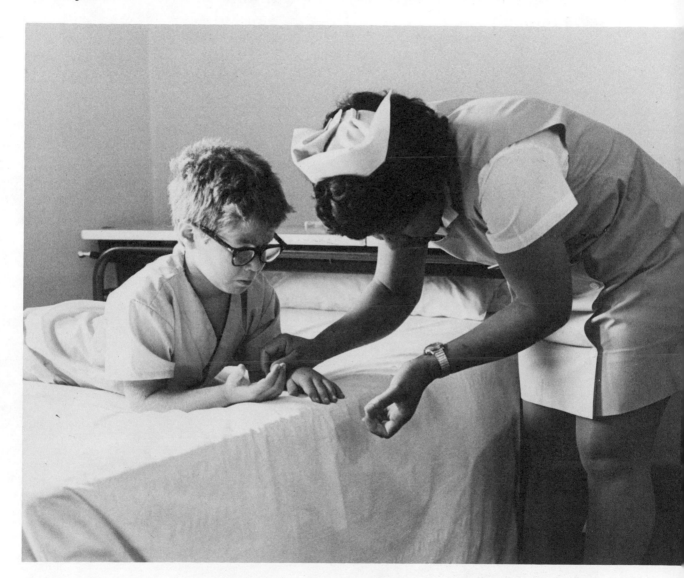

His mother played with him and tried to cheer him up. He was glad she was there with him but he still felt scared and worried.

"I just want to leave the hospital and go home," he said over and over again.

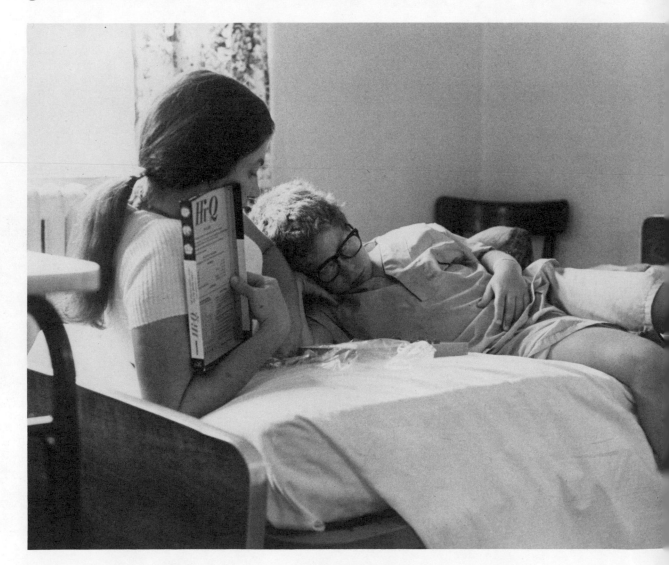

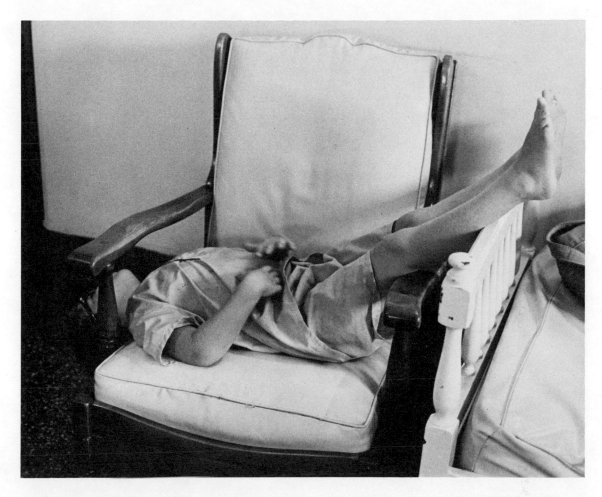

He couldn't seem to keep his mind on
any game.

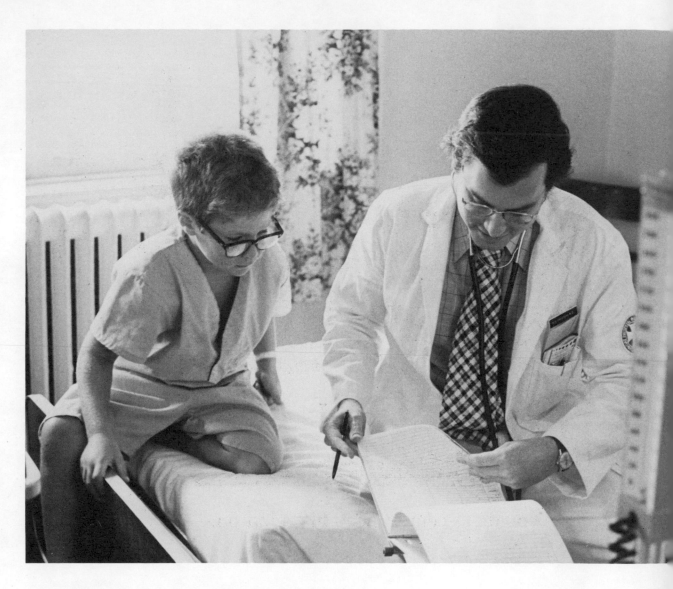

A friendly doctor called a resident
came in and asked a lot of questions.
When Jeff couldn't answer a question,
his mother helped.

The doctor examined Jeff. The
stethoscope was cold on his back and
made him giggle.

"Open up," the doctor said.

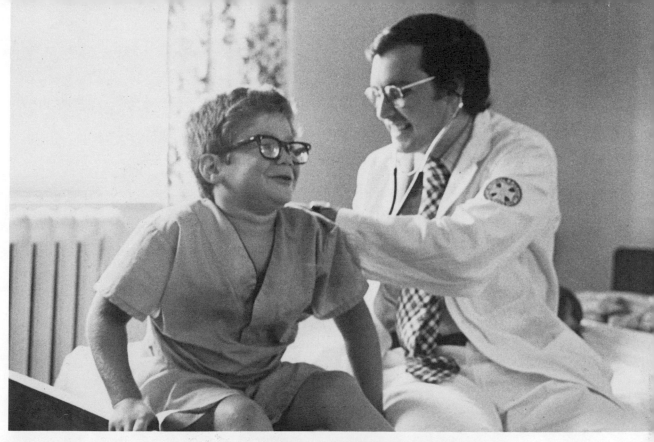
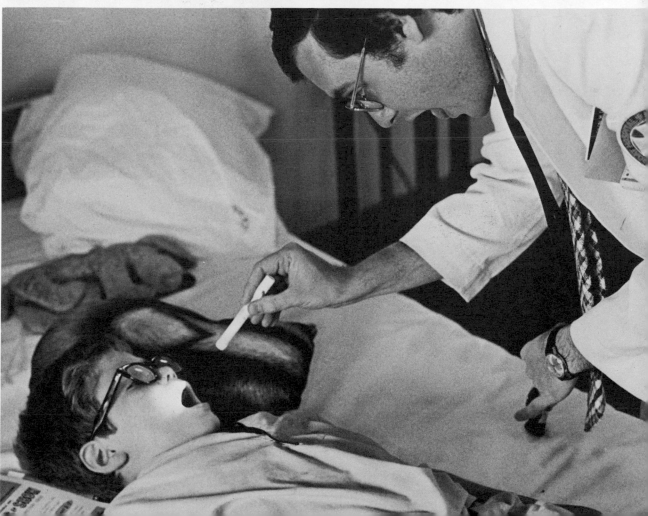

In a few minutes another doctor came in. He said that he was in charge of putting Jeff to sleep for the operation. He was called an anesthesiologist.

Jeff asked him, "How big will my shot be?"

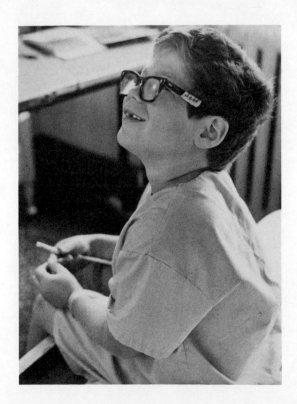

The doctor spread his arms wide and said with a smile, "This big."

Jeff knew the doctor was joking and he smiled too.

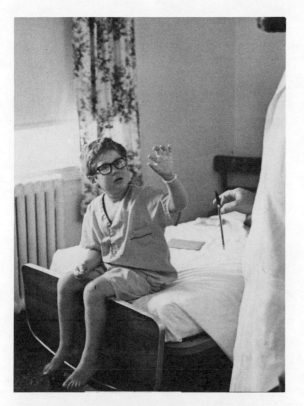

But just to make sure Jeff asked, "Really, how big is the shot?"

The doctor said, "Very little." He also told Jeff not to eat after dinner, so that he would have an empty stomach the next morning when he went for the operation.

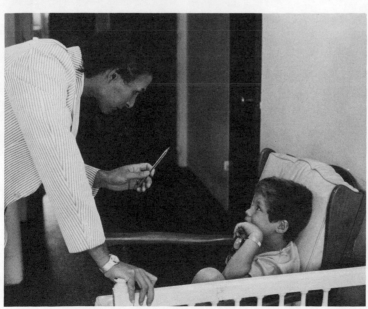

Before bedtime, Jeff's own eye doctor, Dr. Raskind, came to see him.

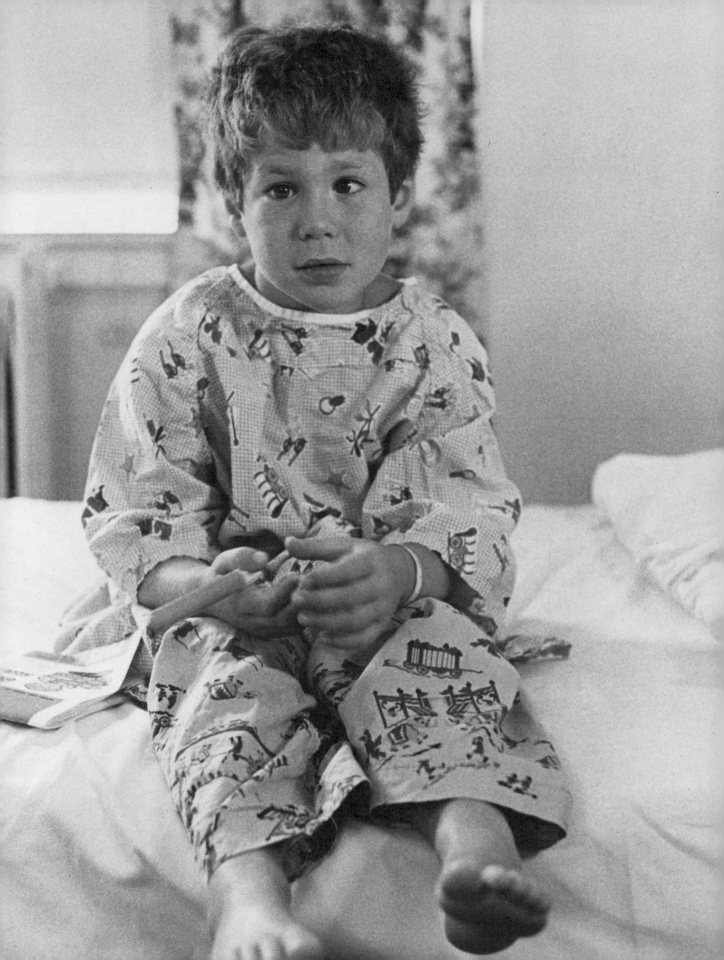

The next morning the nurse brought in some bright clean pajamas for Jeff to put on. She asked him to lie down.

"I'm going to give you something to make you drowsy now. It's not a shot or a pill. It's medicine that slips inside your bottom and goes right to work. It might feel funny, but it won't hurt."

Then she told Jeff to turn over on his tummy. She put in the suppository.

"Now what?" he asked. "Are you going to give me the shot now?"

"Yes," she answered.

"Will it hurt? How far does it go in?"

She told him it was a tiny needle and it would feel like a pinch in the bottom. "Look away," she said.

He counted to five as he felt a tiny pinch.

"That's all," the nurse said.

"Will I have any more?" he asked.

"No," she said.

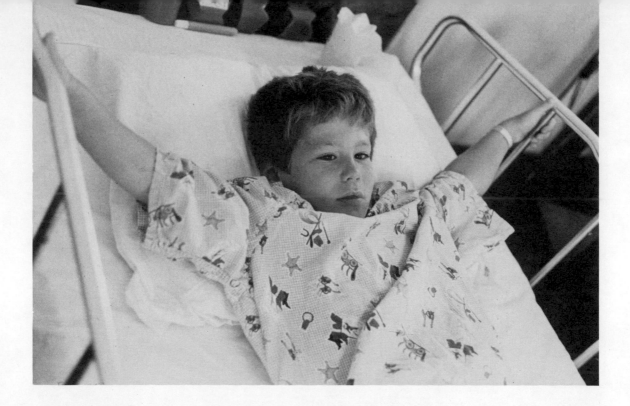

"Why are you pulling up the sides?"
The nurse answered, "You'll be
getting sleepy, and I don't want you to
roll off the bed and get hurt."

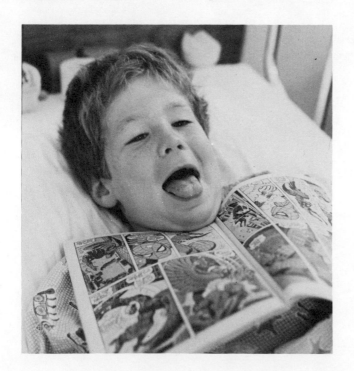

"Why is my mouth
so dry?" he asked.
"There was some-
thing in the shot to dry
up your saliva," the
nurse answered.

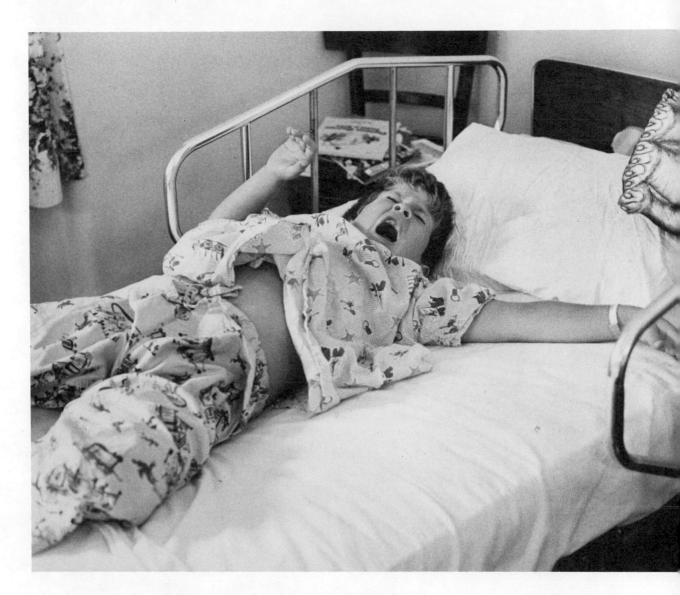

"I'm wide awake," he said, and gave
a big yawn.

"I'm getting sleepy now," he said
softly.

Minutes later, an orderly with a color-
ful hat came in and picked Jeff up.
He said, "How are you, pal?"

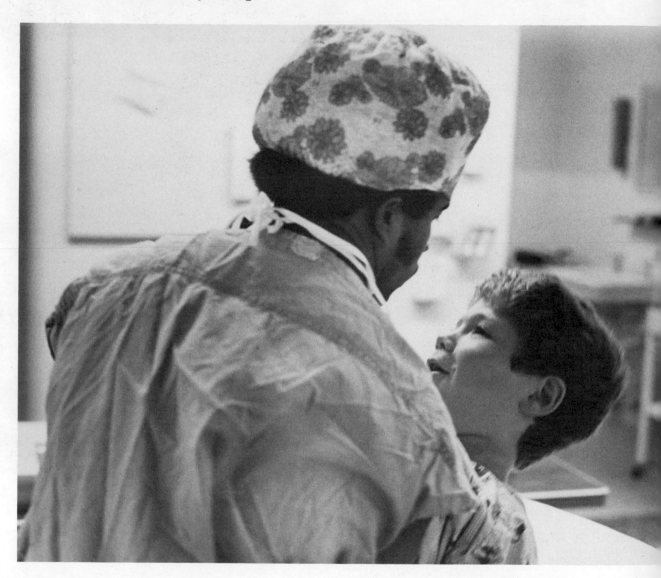

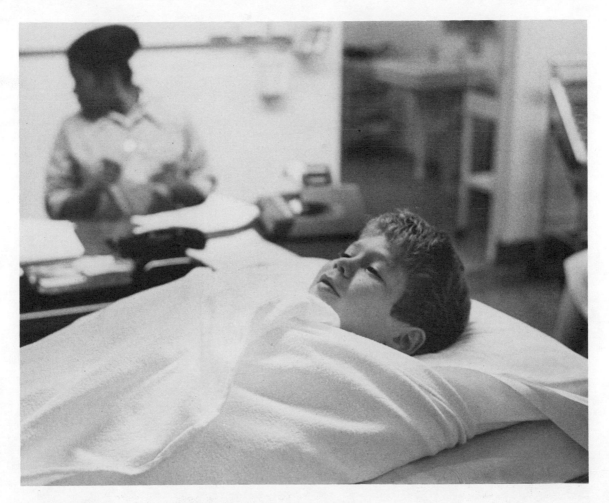

The orderly placed him on a stretcher
and wrapped him up snugly. He put a
canvas belt around him so he wouldn't
fall off the stretcher.

Dr. Raskind stooped over the stretcher
and said hello in the hall outside the
operating room.

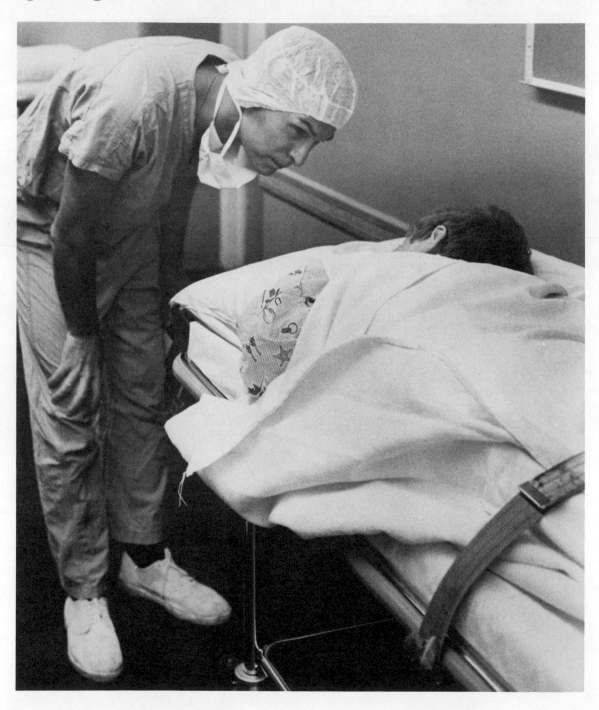

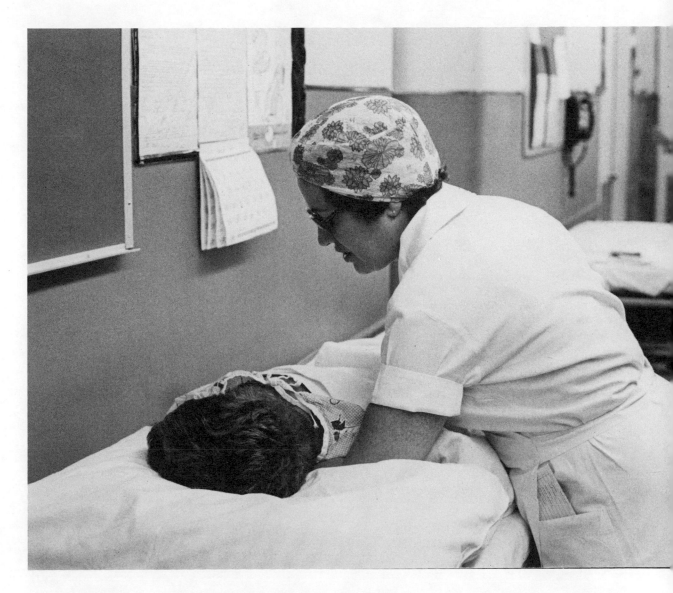

The nurse came over to make sure he was comfortable. She told him to go back to sleep. Soon he would be going into the operating room.

In the operating room, Dr. Raskind put on his mask and checked Jeff's charts once again.

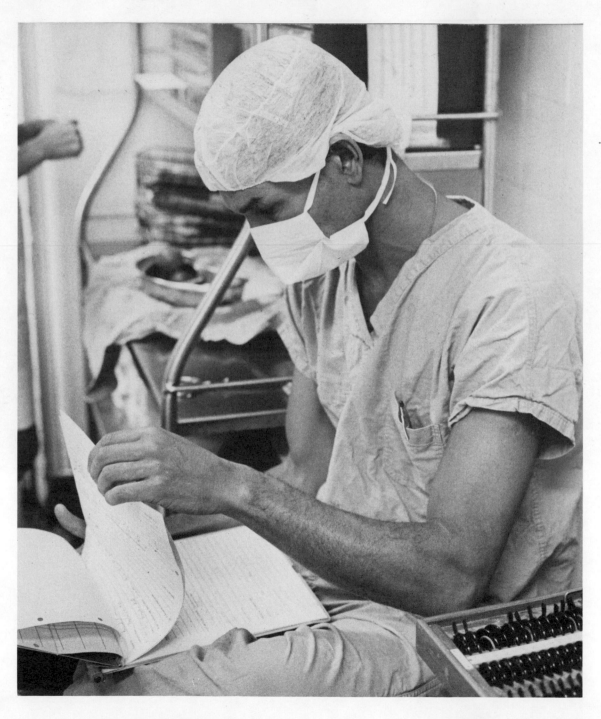

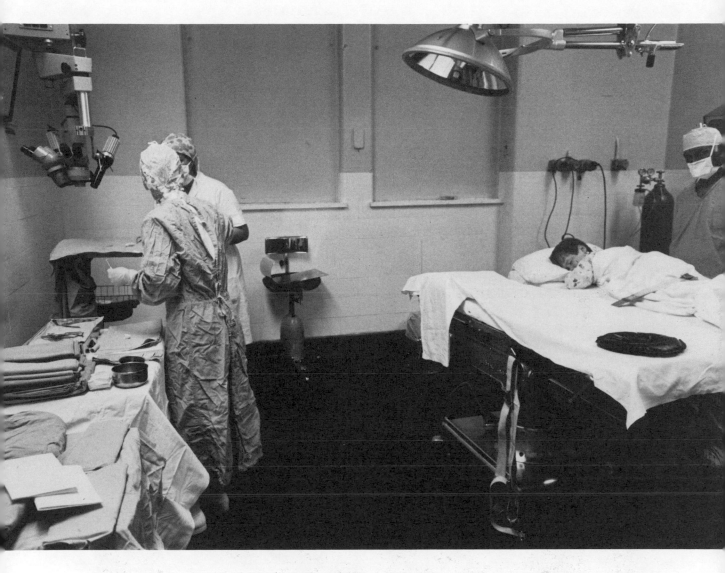

Jeff was fast asleep while the doctors
and nurses prepared themselves for the
operation.

The anesthesiologist put a mask over
Jeff's face after he was asleep. The mask
helped him to breathe gas so he would
stay asleep during the operation.

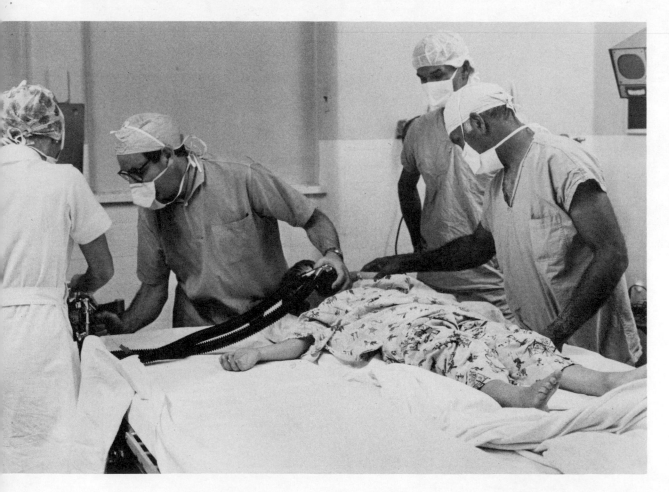

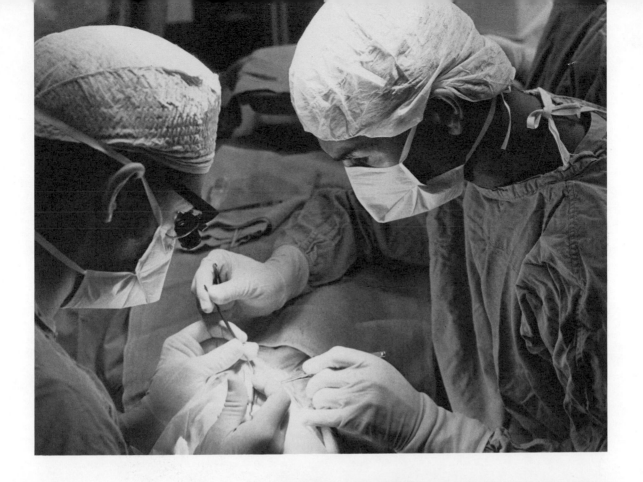

While Jeff was in the operating room his mother was waiting for him in his room.

About an hour later Jeff was in the
recovery room. The nurses stayed with
him while the effect of the gas was
wearing off.

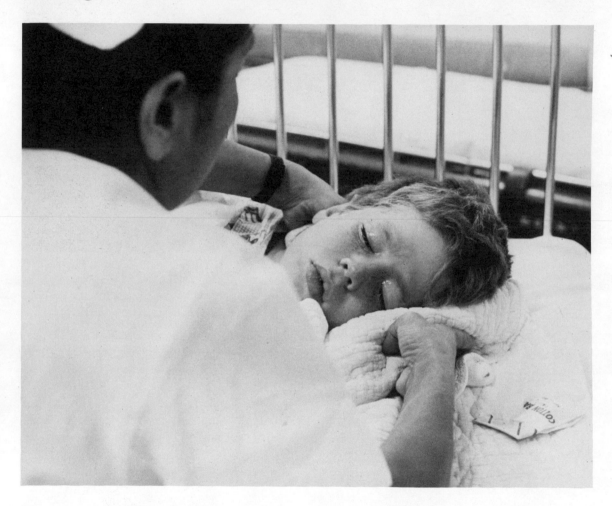

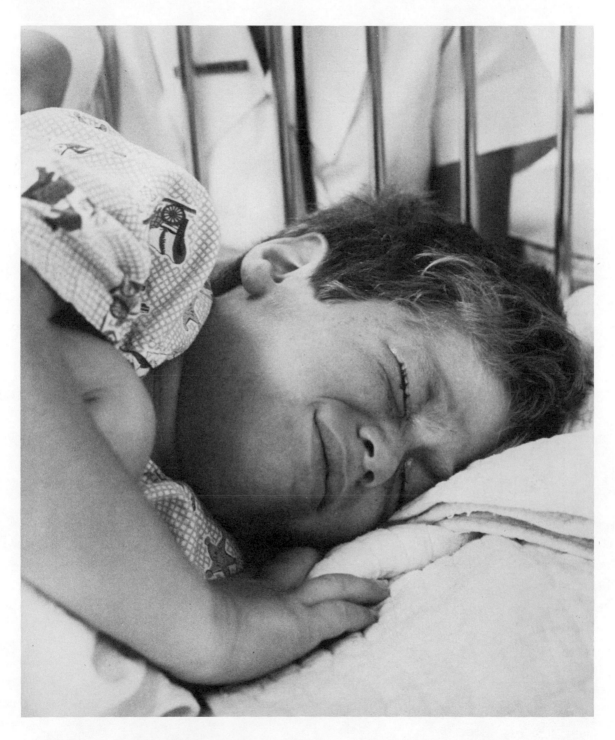

Later he told his mother that his eyes
felt sandy while he was waking up.

When the nurse brought him back to his room, his mother was there. She stayed close to him while he was waking up.

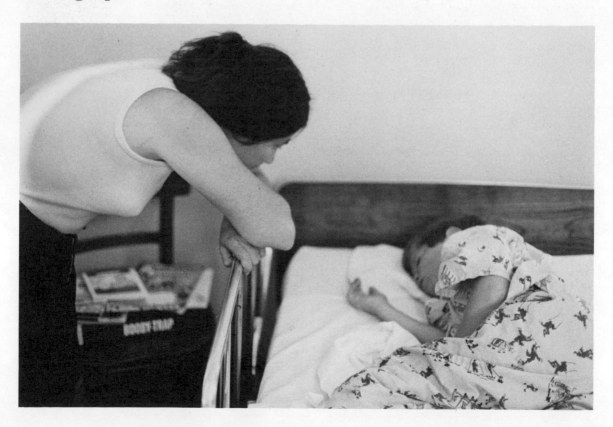

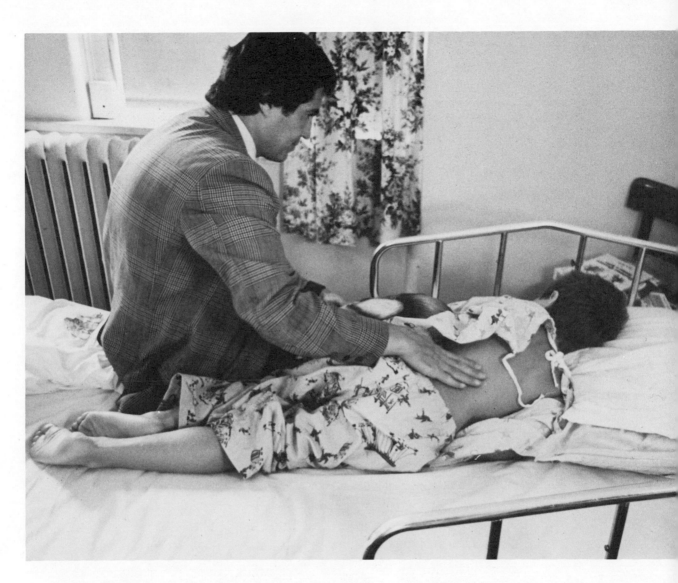

Jeff's daddy was with him after the
operation too.

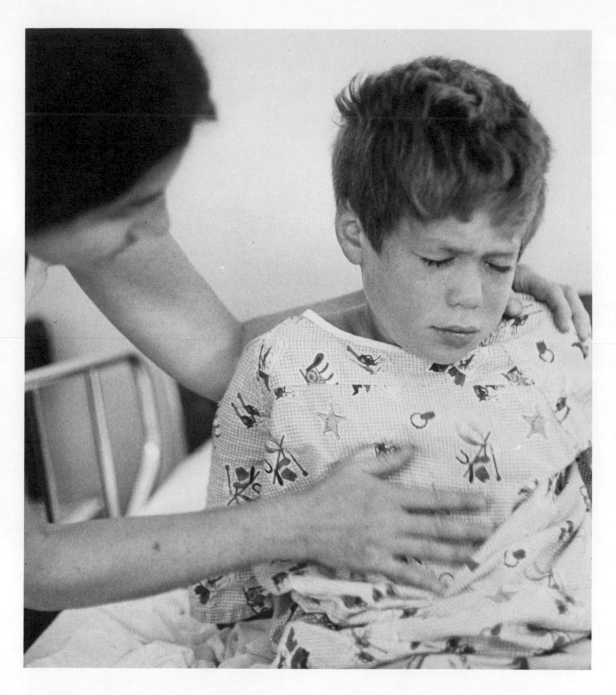

When he tried to sit up, he felt a little
dizzy, so his mother helped him to keep
his balance. It felt good to have her
arms around him.

Dr. Raskind came in to see Jeff.
Jeff was still feeling very drowsy.
Dr. Raskind showed Jeff's mother how
to wipe his eyes with cotton balls if
they stuck together.

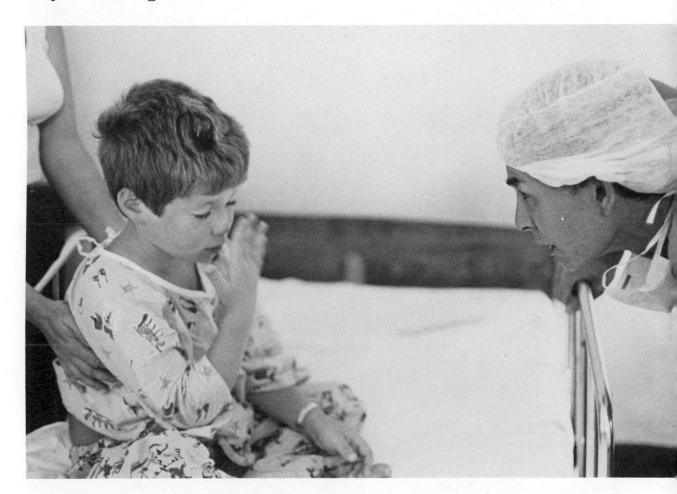

The next morning Jeff's mother wiped
his eyes the way Dr. Raskind had
showed her.

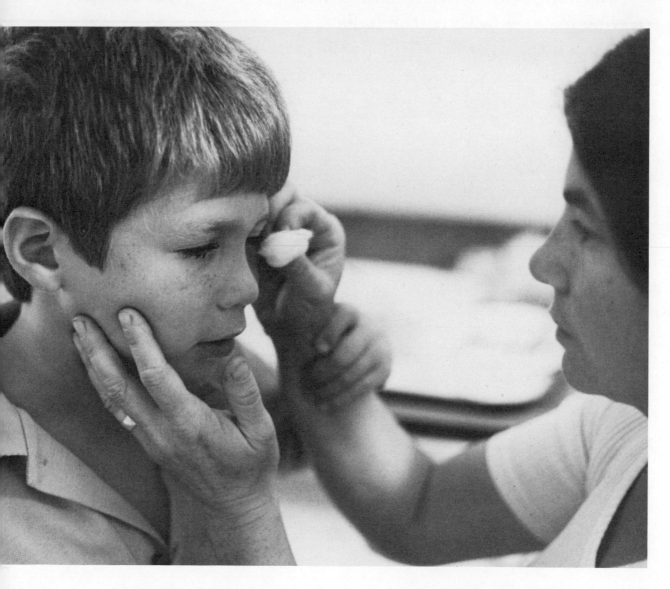

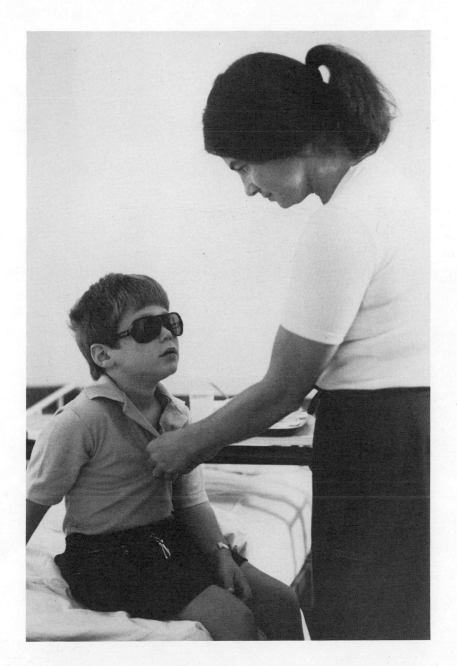

Then she helped Jeff get dressed and asked him if he remembered anything about the operation. All he could remember was being wheeled down the hall on the stretcher.

It was time to go home! Jeff felt
great. He was so happy the operation
was over.

Dr. Raskind told him to wear sun-
glasses for a few days because his eyes
would be sensitive to light.

It was a beautiful day. Jeff was very
happy to be going home.

That afternoon Albert came to play.
Jeff dressed up in the nurse's operating
clothes. He told Albert all about his eye
operation and his stay in the hospital.

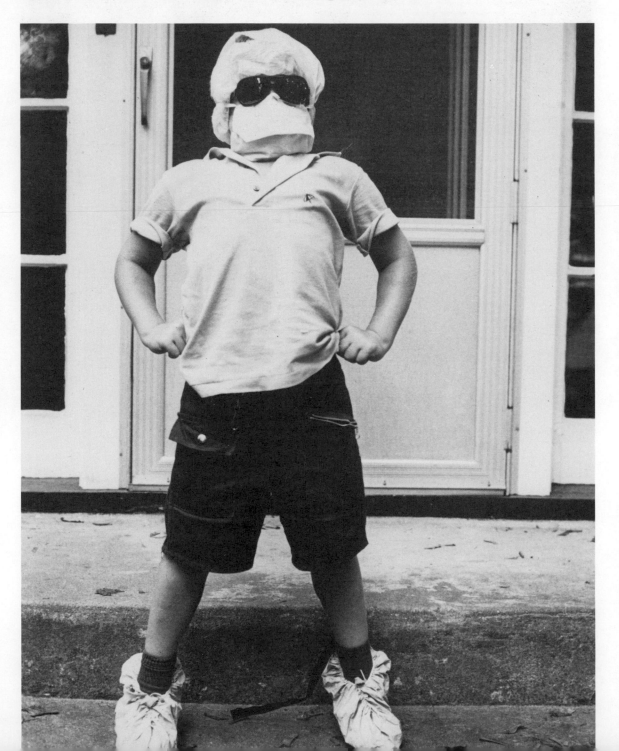

A few weeks later Jeff went to
Dr. Raskind's office for a checkup.
Dr. Raskind said that his eyes were
nice and straight.

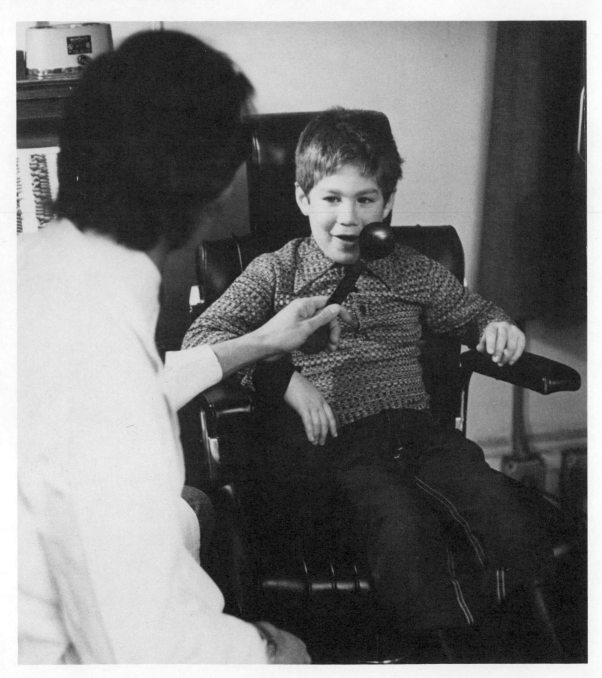